Animaths
Comparing with Cats

Tracey Steffora

Raintree is an imprint of Capstone Global Library Limited, a company incorporated in England and Wales having its registered office at 7 Pilgrim Street, London, EC4V 6LB – Registered company number: 6695582

www.raintreepublishers.co.uk
myorders@raintreepublishers.co.uk

Edited by Daniel Nunn, Abby Colich, and Sian Smith
Designed by Joanna Hinton-Malivoire
Picture research by Elizabeth Alexander
Production by Victoria Fitzgerald
Originated by Capstone Global Library Ltd
Printed and bound in China by Leo Paper Products Ltd

ISBN 978 1 4062 6050 2 (hardback)
17 16 15 14 13
10 9 8 7 6 5 4 3 2 1

ISBN 978 1 4062 6057 1 (paperback)
18 17 16 15
10 9 8 7 6 5 4 3 2

British Library Cataloguing in Publication Data
A full catalogue record for this book is available from the British Library.

Acknowledgements
Shutterstock pp.4, 5, 7, 8, 9, 14, 17, 20 (© Eric Isselee), 4 (© Kirill Vorobyev), 6, 9 (© Iakov Filimonov), 9, 10, 11, 13 (© Katrina Elena), 11, 12, 13 (© Robert Eastman), 12, 13 (© Ultrashock), 15, 17 (© Albie Venter), 16, 17 (© Tatiana Morozova), 18, 19 (© Sari Oneal), 18, 19 (© Stu Porter), 20 (© Viorel Sima), 21 (© Steve Wilson), 21 (© Andreas Gradin); Superstock pp.19 (Gerard Lacz / age fotostock).

Front cover photograph of a kitten reproduced with permission of Shutterstock (© Lana Langlois).
Front cover photograph of a lion and front and back cover photograph of a caracal reproduced with permission of Shutterstock (© Eric Isselée).

We would like to thank Elaine Bennett for her invaluable help in the preparation of this book.

Every effort has been made to contact copyright holders of material reproduced in this book. Any omissions will be rectified in subsequent printings if notice is given to the publisher.

Contents

Comparing cats. 4

Comparing size 6

Comparing weight. 10

Comparing amounts. 14

Comparing speed 18

You compare 20

Cat facts. 22

Glossaries 23

Index 24

Some words are shown in bold, **like this**. You can find them in a glossary on page 23.

Comparing cats

There are many types of cats. Some cats are wild. Some cats are pets. Cats live all over the world. There are many ways cats are alike and different.

We **compare** things to see how they are the same and how they are different. Let's compare some cats!

Comparing size

Look at the **size** of this tiger! Size is how big or small something is. The tiger is the largest of all the cats.

This caracal is also large, but it is smaller than the tiger.

This little kitten is the smallest of all!

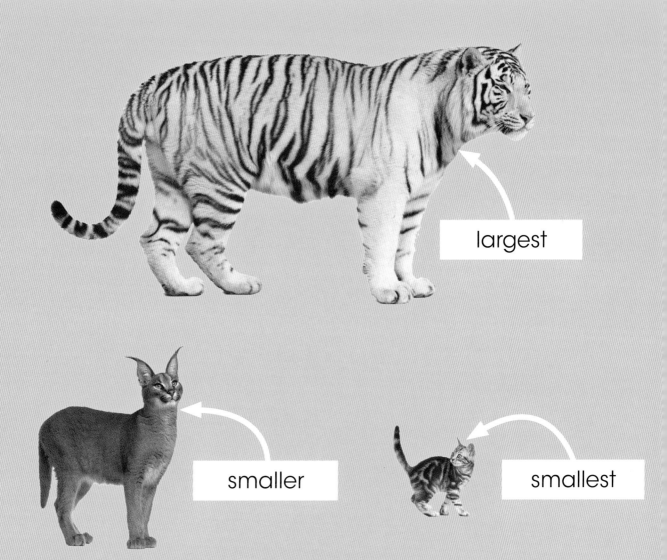

largest

smaller

smallest

Now **compare** the **size** of all three.

Comparing weight

We **weigh** things to find out how heavy they are. Look at this house cat. Its weight is about 5 kilograms.

1 kilogram is about the same weight as a large bag of sugar.

bobcat

This bobcat weighs about 15 kilograms. It is heavier than the house cat.

The cougar **weighs** about 55 kilograms.
It is heavier than the bobcat.

cougar

In fact, it is heavier than the bobcat
and the house cat put together!

Look at the graph

The weight of different animals

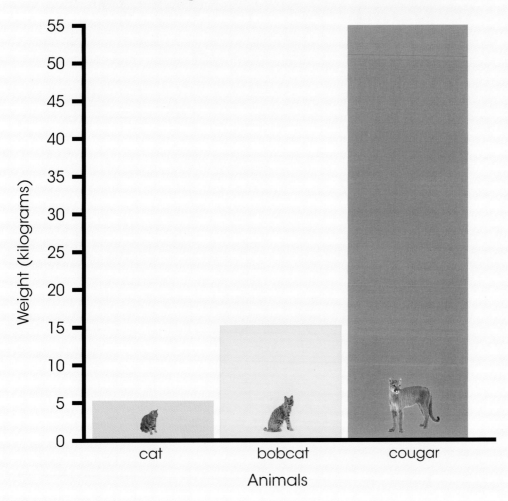

Compare the cats. The house cat is the lightest. The cougar is the heaviest.

Comparing amounts

Now let's **compare** the **amount** of babies in each **litter**. Amount is how many there are of something.

This lynx has a litter of five **cubs**.

This cheetah has a litter of two cubs.

This lioness has a **litter** of three **cubs**.

Look at the graph

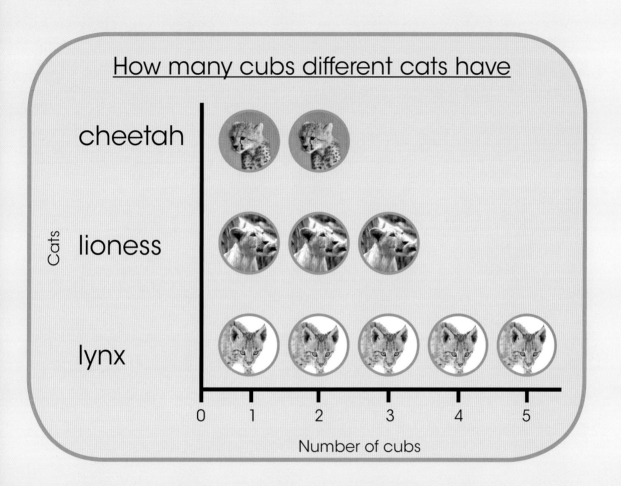

How many cubs different cats have

Cats: cheetah, lioness, lynx

Number of cubs

The lynx has the most cubs.
The cheetah has the fewest cubs.

Comparing speed

Look at this house cat run. It is fast! Its top **speed** is about 30 miles per hour. Speed is how fast or slow something is.

mph stands for miles per hour

This cheetah is much faster! Its top speed is about 70 miles per hour. That is as fast as a car on a motorway!

Look at the graph

The top speed of different animals

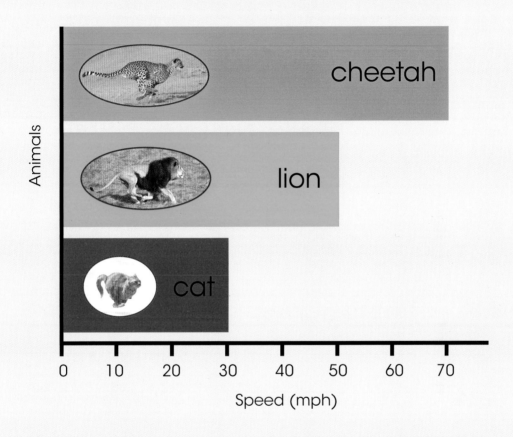

Is the lion faster or slower than the cheetah?

Answer on page 22.

You compare

Which cat is heavier? Which cat is lighter?

house cat

5 kg

65 kg

kg stands for kilograms

leopard

20

jaguar

fishing cat

Which cat is larger?

Which cat is smaller?

Answers on page 22.

Cat facts

- A group of cats is called a clowder.

- All kittens and **cubs** have blue eyes when they are born.

- Cats use their tails to balance and to communicate with each other.

- A cougar is also called a puma, Florida panther, mountain lion, or catamount.

- Only four cats can roar – lions, tigers, leopards, and jaguars!

page 19: The lion is slower than the cheetah. In fact, the cheetah is the fastest animal on land!

page 20: The leopard is heavier. The house cat is lighter.

page 21: The jaguar is larger. The fishing cat is smaller.

Answers

Maths glossary

amount how many there are of something

compare look at two or more things to see how they are the same and how they are different

size how big or small something is

speed how fast or slow something is

weigh to measure how heavy something is

Cat glossary

cub the baby of a big cat, for example a young lion or a young tiger

litter a group of baby animals that are born at the same time

Index

amount 14, 23

compare 4, 5, 6, 9, 13, 14, 18, 20, 23

cubs 14, 15, 16, 17, 22, 23

graphs 13, 17, 19

heavy 10, 11, 12, 13, 20

light 13, 20

litters 14, 15, 16, 23

pets 4

size 6, 9, 23

speed 18, 19

weight 10, 11, 12, 13, 23

wild 4